Thirty-one Days

BEFORE the THRONE

A CALL TO PRAYER

I saw the Lord, high and exalted, seated on a throne, and the train of his robe filled the temple.
Isaiah 6:1

As you continue seeking God's face and favor, may you find answers in the asking, knowledge in the kneeling, great joy in the journeying, the power of the Spirit in your praying, and the presence of Christ in your living!

Judy Van Hemert Hunt

ISBN: 0615964605
ISBN-13: 9780615964607

FOREWORD

In Matthew's gospel, Jesus calls his listeners to be intentional about prayer, to "go into your room and shut the door" and to refrain from empty phrases. But often when we're alone in our room with the door shut, it's too easy for our minds to drift or our eyes to close—not in reverence, but in sleep!

Thirty-One Days Before the Throne is a guide for those of us who know we need prayer in our life. We want to pray but somehow lack the discipline or the tools to begin again—or for the first time.

This guide is the perfect starting point for a lifelong commitment to time alone with God. With each new day, there are suggestions for scripture reading, questions to help reflect upon those passages and their application to your real-world life, and a place for recording your insights and God's voice. The day's devotional time concludes with a prayer that can be prayed as is or used as a springboard for your personal or intercessory prayers.

Thirty-One Days Before the Throne is an ideal guide for individuals, small groups, or for use in a care-giving, one-on-one relationship where assurance of God's presence is sought. Whether you find yourself with a song in your heart or a lump in your throat, any time is the perfect time to turn your face toward God's merciful throne.

Day 1

READ: Psalm 139:1-18, 23-24

REFLECT:
How are you attempting to hide from yourself?
From your God?
How can the Psalmist's recognition of God's constant
    presence serve as an encouragement for you?
How can God's light banish your darkness today?
Who else needs to be made aware of the Light?

RECORD:

_____

_____

_____

_____

_____

_____

_____

_____

_____

_____

_____

PRAY:

O Holy and merciful God, thank you for welcoming me into your throne room this day. Thank you for the certainty that you *delight* in my presence and in my invitation for you to join me in this journey. But where else could I go, Lord? For, even in the midst of my God-moments, this week has brought disappointment, frustration, conflict, unwanted news, and unresolved struggles. So I come to you, not as a heavenly vending machine, but because you have *invited* me as your child to prayer. And in that invitation, I can be confident that when I'm so torn that I don't even know *how* to pray, your Holy Spirit will carry my deepest needs straight before that throne of grace.

May I take seriously the power that's released when I call upon you to banish darkness, bind up the broken, and embolden those who falter. And, may I be used—not as a religious battering ram, but as a believer who falls to my knees that others might be raised up.

Gracious God, remind me that it's not my posture, but my persistence in prayer that you long for. Not formulas, but faithfulness and intentionality in recognizing your constant presence in my life. Help me know that I'm not called to make sense of this nonsensical world, but to trust in you—not only voicing my anger, concerns, fear, *and* praise, but also taking the time to *listen* as you reply. For, God, it's not a prayer life that I need, but a life of prayer; a constant and consistent conversation that strengthens and deepens my relationship with you.

So, with your disciples then and now, I cry out, "Teach me to pray..."   Amen.

Day 2

READ: 2 Corinthians 5:16-21

REFLECT:
How will I live a resurrected life today?
How will I see the "new creation" in people I encounter—
particularly those I don't like or with whom I disagree?

RECORD:

_____

_____

_____

_____

_____

_____

_____

_____

_____

_____

_____

_____

_____

_____

_____

_____

PRAY:

Holy God, with shouts of "He is risen, indeed!" we continue to celebrate the greatest story ever told. We rejoice in YOUR victory over death and the promise that it holds for us. And I want so badly to comply when I hear those words, "Come, follow me." Truly, I desire to walk the path you so lovingly and wisely set before us. Then, I discover following also means setting aside my callous thoughts and self-centered ways—giving up *my* understanding and the council of those with hidden agendas. You long to raise me to new life, but *I* prefer the entanglements and self-pronounced infallible insights of the old. So, each day becomes a battle of the wills, and each day I wonder at the lack of victory and joy in my life. Lord, open my eyes to the fallacy of my ways—to the reality that surrender is the sure way to success; and that by following *your* lead, I am led into decisions and directions that glorify you and bring me a peace that passes all understanding.

Gracious God, in your mercy now bind up the wounds of the brokenhearted; restore relationships; provide comfort and healing to those who battle disease and infirmity. Through me, provide hope, encouragement, and love to those whom others have forgotten. Protect those who protect us and hold back the forces of self-serving war until peace—not violence—becomes the norm.

Bless what will be offered to others this day in your name and in thanksgiving for the simple truth that all I have is simply a gift from you. Use me to your glory as you use each of your followers to carry your message of resurrected and abundant life into your world that longs for new creation.

In Jesus' name. Amen.

Day 3

READ: I Corinthians 12:1, 7-14

REFLECT:

Every believer is given at least one spiritual gift.

Do you know what your spiritual gifts are? If not, there are several on-line inventories to help you. Take some time today to discover your gifts.

How will you use your gifts today? This week? In working with others as a part of Christ's body?

RECORD:

PRAY:

Lord, I'm fractured and I'm torn. Sorrows assail me, tragedies lie all around me. Wars and rumors of wars permeate the air waves. And, too often, our lives seem to be a battleground as we struggle against one another. But, that's not the life you envision for any of us, nor the life to which you call me. So in this moment, help me to cease striving. Calm my spirit, quiet my rushing mind. Help me to breathe deeply of your Spirit. And, in this hour, remind me that beyond the gift of salvation, it has been your good pleasure to endow each of your followers also with *spiritual* gifts—gifts not to be hoarded—not to feel superior, but so we might dwell and work together in community with one another and in *communion* with you. For these unique capabilities and our physical and financial attributes were not meant to divide us, but to help us recognize our need for one another.

So may I freely choose to live in the way you intended: building something good and pleasing in your sight, rather than my own little empire. Help me catch the vision of what can be created in *your* name—a vision of inclusion, peace and joy. And, remind me that your call is to unity, not uniformity, because what we create together will always far surpass what we can accomplish in isolation. For in your economy, O God, we are each essential to the realization of your plan that your kingdom *will* come upon this earth. So help me see the possibilities, and bless my efforts to share my God-given resources. Even as I offer up tangible signs of my love and gratitude this day, take my desire to live according to your will and multiply my commitment to cooperation. May I discover your paradoxical truth that it is only in giving my gifts and myself away, that the pieces of my life are truly made whole.

This I pray with confidence in Jesus' name. Amen.

Day 4

READ: Isaiah 61:1-3
       Psalm 51:10-13

REFLECT:

    What is in need of restoration in your life today?
    What beauty has God given in place of the ashes of despair?

RECORD:

PRAY:

Holy God, I've come to meet you in this place. Intentionally, I've come seeking your presence, your touch, your acceptance. In spite of all that surrounds me, I've come to spend time with you. Thank you for this sanctuary—for this place of safety and refuge; for this time of encounter and straight talk; for you promise that you will never leave or forsake me.

Yet, Lord, I know there are other meeting places. That you wait for me in unexpected locations and in unanticipated ways. So help me recognize your voice in those times and places. When I hear you call, may I jump to serve, rather than jumping to conclusions. As I surrender to your will, may I be willing to *truly* hear what you ask of me.

God of all nations, as I consider your place in this country, I must confess that we fall far short of your will. So, I call on you to move within this nation and *all* nations to bring about understanding, reconciliation, and peace. I pray your will would be done in the lives and decisions of our leaders, and that they would be drawn to trust in you alone, rather than leaning on their own understanding. I pray for those who are persecuted for the color of their skin, their beliefs, their heritage, and I look toward the day when relationships are transformed, instead, by the power of your Spirit and the message of the One who came to seek and save us all, Jesus Christ our Lord.

This is my prayer as I pray in that blessed name. Amen.

Day 5

READ: Romans 7:14-8:2

REFLECT:

What are those things to which you have become a slave?

From what is God longing to set you free?

What is one thing you will do today that is pleasing in God's sight?

How will the truth that you are created in God's image help you make right choices today?

RECORD:

PRAY:

Lord, you call us to journey with you on this road called life. And it's a journey that's to be marked by love: love of God, of neighbor and of self. But too frequently, I've chosen to veer off that narrow path, finding instead an alluring detour to a road strewn with jealousy, self-advancement, anger, intolerance, and sometimes, even hatred. I have cleverly disguised my ulterior motives behind a cloak of saccharine sweetness. At times, I even act as if I love myself more than others. Yet, if the truth were told, way too often, I really don't like myself much at all. Like the Apostle Paul, the things I *would* do, I leave undone, rushing instead, headlong into those things I know to be hurtful and harmful. So, guide me from this path of cheap thrills and point me, instead, to the reality that a true joyride can be found only when you are my traveling companion. Remind me that you are the embodiment of love, and it is in your image that I have been created—created *worthy* of receiving and giving genuine, selfless love.

Lord, bless those separated from loved ones by distance or death, and those who serve to protect us here and around the world. Use me to encourage those whose hope grows dim and to eradicate the maladies of disease, poverty, intolerance, and injustice. Use me today in ways that lead others to be drawn to your love and mercy, simply by the ways I choose to travel this life in Christian love.

This is my prayer as I pray through the strength of Jesus. Amen.

Day 6

READ: Psalm 22:1-2; 19-31

REFLECT:
When has God rescued you?
How does God want to use your current circumstances to
    draw you closer?
How will you testify to God's love?

RECORD:

_____
_____
_____
_____
_____
_____
_____
_____
_____
_____
_____
_____
_____
_____
_____

PRAY:

Gracious and Holy God, I enter your presence this morning to thank you for what you have so generously given me—mercy upon mercy and blessing upon blessing. Thank you, Lord, because I also come to bring you my broken pieces—my unmet expectations, my considerable losses, my raw emotions, and those questions that seem to have no end.

Scarcely able to comprehend all that is going on in my own life, I see others who find themselves in the midst of turmoil and tragedy as well. Day after day, our sight is assailed by sensationalism; our ears hear the cries of anger and anguish; our hearts are wrenched by questions that go unanswered. Daily, we contend with crises that are played out all around us.

Yet, even in the midst of so much uncertainty—so much confusion—your love still triumphs! For those sights and sounds, those lasting impressions of tragic events, also reveal that which is best within us and our communities. Sacrificial love, Christ-like love, continues to prevail when we disregard our own safety to rescue others; when strangers provide solace; when an outpouring of prayers surrounds and lifts me and all those in need. Through these responses, help me recognize the truth that we weren't made for isolation—that we truly need one another, not just for commerce, but for community. Remind me again that our lives are integrally intertwined so that one is not complete until we *all* are, and no one is truly victorious until *all* of your creation experiences victory in living and in loving. Continue to raise up those who seek to understand, rather than being understood; who desire to hear, rather than to be heard; who give their very lives away so that others might live. And, gracious God, raise *me* to new life that it might be said, "See how God has worked another miracle!"

Hear my prayer for Jesus' sake. Amen.

Day 7

READ: Genesis 1:1-2:2

REFLECT:

YOU are made in God's image!

God has called YOU "very good!"

How does God want to use you as a co-creator?

RECORD:

_____

_____

_____

_____

_____

_____

_____

_____

_____

_____

_____

_____

_____

_____

_____

PRAY:

Creator God, by the labor of your hands you formed us from the void and called us very good. And in the rhythm of your creation, you rested. Not from exhaustion but as an example for us who are made in your image. When you delivered your people from bondage, you called us to Sabbath rest, a rest in which we remember all your mercies so that we might keep the day holy and set apart for you. Yet, O God, we've lost sight of that command, just as sometimes, we lose sight of you. So I thank you for calling me back this day; for inhabiting my worship; for drawing near to me as I seek to draw near to you.

Lord, as I approach this day knowing there is work ahead for me—work that may never be recognized by anyone but you—I give you thanks for those who make a difference in *my* life. For farmers and merchants, for tradespeople and those who serve me in quiet and unassuming ways. Bless those mothers and fathers, grandparents, teachers, and mentors whose tireless labor of love makes a difference in the lives of so many children. Protect those who safeguard me from others, and sometimes from myself. Pour out your mercy on those who seek gainful employment and on the ones who are *under*employed or exploited by others. May they have the courage to persevere and may you provide a way when there seems to be none at all.

Gracious God, as I offer to you the fruit of this day's labor, remind me that I am simply your steward, called to be faithful and generous with what you have entrusted to me; called to use my time and talents under your guidance. By the power of your Holy Spirit direct my steps so that at the end of this day, I might rest in the knowledge that I have been used to your glory as a co-creator of your kingdom here on earth.

This is my prayer, prayed in the name of Jesus. Amen.

Day 8

READ: Romans 12:1-5

REFLECT:
Who do I need to see as an equal?
Who is God calling me to see through *Godly* eyes?
To whom do I need to speak a word of forgiveness?
Are there changes I need to make in what I'm feeding my
mind?

RECORD:

PRAY:

Loving Lord, you call us into relationships because you declare it's not good for us to be alone. As Father, Son, and Spirit are connected, so you have designed *us* to be connected, interdependent, needing one another to accomplish the purpose for which we were created. You give us the gift of family that we might have a source of nurture and love. Yet, too often, I'm so focused on having my own needs met that I lash out at what I don't understand; withdraw from unpleasant circumstances; abdicate my role as the one designed to set a positive example as guide, protector, peacemaker. Therefore, I enter the larger family—the family of God—the Body of Christ with old habits, deep-seated wounds, mistrust, and anger rooted in fear. My words become degrading and my actions belie the fact that I am a follower of Christ. Yet, it is in his very example that I find hope—for in you, Lord, I can experience forgiveness and learn what it means to forgive others. In your Word, I can read about changed lives and know that's a possibility for me, too. And, all around me, I can participate in transforming acts and experience the truth that I am not called to conform to this world and its unhealthy ways of living, but to be *transformed* by the renewing of my mind.

My prayer today then, O Lord, is that you will give me clear vision to see what I've become; courage to take that first step toward a life that mirrors yours; and great desire to give myself away so that this world, my community, my family might more closely resemble what you intended.

This I pray in Jesus' name. Amen.

$\mathcal{D}ay$ 9

READ: Psalm 51:1-17

REFLECT:
    For what do you need to ask forgiveness today?
    How will you take God's promise of forgiveness to heart?
    How will you express the "joy of God's salvation" in the way
        you speak and live today?

RECORD:

PRAY:
God of new beginnings, you pick up the pieces of our lives. Calling us to remember the lessons of the past, you *re*-member us—you put us back together, connecting us with others who have walked the path of brokenness, loss, and sorrow. You give us strength for today and hope for tomorrow, and then you call us forward, giving us *everything* we will need for this new leg of our journey. So, place in my eyes *your* vision and deep within my heart *your* song of mercy and of miraculous possibilities.

As the seasons begin to change from winter to spring, from spring to summer, and from summer to fall, may I fall more in love with you, slowing my pace, taking time to listen for your voice and *your* will. Today, I ask your blessing on the students of this community and of others, Lord, students of all ages, students of academics, of life, and of your Word. Particularly, I pray for those who find themselves in new and scary surroundings. Bless those who teach that they might not only impart the subject matter, but your love, grace, and truth as well. And, bless me as I boldly step into your future, learning your ways and building something beautiful and of eternal importance. This day, loving Lord, use my uniquely God-given gifts, my very life so that in the community of faith we might truly accomplish even greater things in your name and to your glory.

God of all creation, create in *me* something beautiful; something so unique and spectacular that others are edified and you are glorified. Then, through your example, teach me the truth that it takes each of us and all of us dying to ourselves in order that we might live totally and completely for you.

Hear my prayer and be my Teacher, Jesus. Amen.

$\mathscr{D}ay\ 10$

READ: II Chronicles 7:13-20
Colossians 3:16-17

REFLECT:
What can I do today that will make a difference?
For whom should I be praying?
What words and songs of praise and encouragement will I
offer today?

RECORD:

_____
_____
_____
_____
_____
_____
_____
_____
_____
_____
_____
_____
_____
_____

PRAY:

Gracious God, your Word declares that we are to offer petitions, prayers, intercession and thanksgiving for all those in authority, so I lift to you today our nation's leaders. Lord, I pray for our President, legislators, and judicial leaders; for the men and women who have been elected to represent and serve us, *and* for those who influence the decisions of our representatives. I pray, Holy God, that each might be guided by your Holy Spirit and have the courage to move under your Spirit's direction, rather than their own. I pray that partisanship would be transformed into a spirit of cooperation and an overriding desire to ensure equitable outcomes; that relationships with other nations would be guided by the understanding that we are all God's children—called to be stewards and to dwell in peace so far as it is possible, rather than repaying evil for evil. Lord, I ask that you would surround these national, state, and local leaders with your hedge of protection, not only from *physical* harm, but from those temptations that come with great power; from those lures of small steps in the wrong direction that lead to greater missteps; from their sense of isolation to a place of safe collaboration; and from a feeling of entitlement into a life of selfless service.

Lord, hear my prayers; come and heal our land that this day would bring forth a *new* beginning, one through which our nation would be strengthened by the leadership of those in authority, and one in which these United States would truly become united in our desire to love and serve you as we love and serve *all* those you place before us. Today, let there be peace on earth. Today, gracious God, let it begin with me.

In your holy name and by your holy power I pray. Amen.

Day 11

READ: 1 Timothy 6:6-19
Proverbs 3:5-6

REFLECT:

Righteousness means doing the right thing at the right time for the right reasons.

What do I need to flee *from* in order to run *toward* righteousness?

In *what* and *whom* am I trusting?

How has my heart become hardened and cold? When have I experienced that "strangely warmed" feeling of God's presence in my life?

Am I willing to seek its return as I invite the Holy Spirit to fill me that I might be emptied of myself?

RECORD:

PRAY:

Holy God, I tumble into this season of my life so preoccupied with the rat race, my routines, the rush of days, that my attention is everywhere but on my righteousness. And then, nature steps in to remind me just how powerless I truly am. Empty streets bring to mind how empty my life is without you. The starkness of a wintry scene speaks to me of how barren my existence can be without your presence in my life. The dried, summer grass becomes a perfect image of my parched spirit. So, Lord, as I survey that life, may I see the folly of leaning on my own understanding, and trust instead in *you* with all my heart. In bleak midwinter scenes may I be reminded of the men, women, and children who shiver in the cold—those who have no actual or metaphorical shelter; those who hunger and thirst for literal and spiritual food. And in the oppression of a sultry summer night, bring to mind those who seek justice and peace for themselves and others. Then, may I come to the realization that through *you* I hold the resources needed; those resources that can provide refuge, sustenance, fairness, harmony. For the truth is, I don't need to be taught the right thing, I simply have to have the courage to *do* what is right. To speak and act in ways that lead to reconciliation, restoration, and a returning to the abundance of your grace.

Give me that courage, gracious God, so that the burn of anger might be quenched, the chill of man's inhumanity to man might be transformed by the warmth of selfless love, and darkness might be dispelled by your Holy Light. Take my life this day and use it for that transformation. Take me and put me to work as your agent of Godly change.

For this is my prayer, Lord. A prayer offered in Jesus' precious name. Amen.

Day 12

READ: Matthew 28:16-20
          John 13:31-35

REFLECT:

When you have good news, who do you tell and how?

The word "evangelism" comes from the Greek *evangelon* which simply means good news. It has been said that evangelism is nothing more than one beggar telling another beggar where to find bread.[1] How might this change your attitude about being and "evangelist"?

When have you followed Jesus' command to go into your world and share the good news of what he has done for you?

When have you demonstrated that you are a disciple by showing love?

How might the way you love someone today become a telling of the Good News?

RECORD:

_____

_____

_____

_____

_____

_____

_____

---

1   D. T. Niles

PRAY:

Loving Lord, as I join you today, bring to my mind all those who have met me at the point of need: those who shared with me the great Good News of your life, death, and resurrection; those who came into the ends of *my* world and taught me your Word and your ways. What a life-changing gift they each have been. Can that be said of me? In what ways have *I* been your disciple who has loved and sought out others, telling of your gift of grace, issuing an invitation into the family of God, giving of myself in ways that reflected your life? Would you give me a glimpse of those moments as well?

Precious Savior, would you remind me how easy and joyful it is to simply speak forth all the ways you have changed my life? For surely you have found me in dark places and moved me into the light; taken my brokenness and mended it with your love; found my rough edges and polished them with your tender, nail-scarred hands. You have fed me at your holy table, set me free by your cup of forgiveness, and led me in right paths by the gentle whisper of your Holy Spirit. How can I keep these miracles only for myself? How can I hoard what you have so freely given?

Today, let me be bold; let me be wise; let me be brimming with generosity in the way I offer your love to others. Maybe it's just a word, a wink, a smile. Perhaps, you'll send me someone who needs more than that. But in the smallest of ways—and in the grandest— let me present your Good News to everyone I encounter this day. Today, may I be your evangelist!

This is my prayer. Amen.

Day 13

READ: Lamentations 3:21-23
Psalm 40:1-10

REFLECT:
How has God's faithfulness been evident in your life this
week?
This month?

RECORD:

_____
_____
_____
_____
_____
_____
_____
_____
_____
_____
_____
_____
_____
_____

PRAY:

Faithful God, what better way to begin this new day than to step into your presence as I come to worship you? Truly, I'm eager to say good-bye to my yesterdays—to dismiss their tragedies and disappointments. But before I step upon this fresh, unmarked path that lies before me, I want to pause to give thanks for your faithfulness. Faithfulness that has been clothed in those who took time to make that unexpected phone call, offer a much-needed, gentle hug, share an outpouring of love and support. Again and again, you have proven your love in the releasing of guilt, gifts of generosity, unanticipated solutions, and even through unanswered prayers. In these and all things may I recognize your guiding and sustaining hand, and remember your surrounding love at every time and place of my life. In that recognition, I pray that I will begin to grasp how wide and long—how high and deep your love truly is. May that knowledge give me the courage to embark with renewed strength upon this day's adventure to which you call me.

Lord, I pray for the battlefield of the minds within our children and students and for *all* places of conflict where lives are forever changed. I speak peace upon our military and upon those who would seek to destroy freedom. I speak healing upon those who are entrapped by physical, mental, and spiritual maladies—and upon this nation. And, I speak reconciliation upon those who run from one another and from you.

Lord, fill me with your Spirit that I might move in the power of your light and love today and in the days ahead. According to your Word, use me in ways that are immeasurably more than all I ask or imagine. This day I relinquish my life into your hands and for your glory.

This I pray in Jesus' name. Amen.

Day 14

READ: Proverbs 31:10-31

REFLECT:

What is your favorite hymn? Take time now to sing it to the Lord.

What truth do you find in Proverbs 31?

Who has been like a mother to you? Give God thanks for that relationship…and let her know!

RECORD:

PRAY:

Gracious God, I need this time with you—time to step into this relationship—time to worship you in song and word and deed. For I have caught a glimpse of your great love for me in the eyes of my mother; felt the comfort of your gentle spirit in the tender touch of her hand, and known a hope that endures all things simply because she believed in me. So, today in thanksgiving, I lift before you the gift of mothers. Mothers, who by birth or by your divine intervention have loved and sacrificed, guided my steps and pointed me toward you. Thank you for women who have given of themselves and asked little in return. And thank you for men who have been thrust into the mothering role, casting aside society's convention. Thank you for that remembrance of the faithful cloud of moms who even now cheers me on from a more distant place.

Bless and undergird *all* mothers. Give courage to those who struggle to provide for their children; provide healing to the one who struggles with post-partum depression; peace to the mother who has lovingly placed her child for adoption; hope for those mothers who have outlived son or daughter; reconciliation for those estranged from their children; and Godly wisdom for all mothers everywhere who unconditionally love through thick and thin. Teach me to forgive their inadequacies as they have had to forgive my stubborn streaks, rebellion, and lack of respect. And, help me recognize the truth that a mother, a gift so very precious, could only have been created by your design.

With a grateful heart and in Jesus' name I pray. Amen.

Day 15

READ: Luke 6:43-49
         Matthew 6:19-21

REFLECT:

   Where is your heart today?
   What "treasures" are you withholding from God?
   How are you living in *God's* abundance?

RECORD:

PRAY:

Gracious God, your Word declares that a good person brings forth good things out of the good stored up in their heart. For the mouth *speaks* of what has filled the heart. And, I know that extends to my giving as well. For when my heart is filled with gratitude for the abundance of good you shower upon me; when my soul is touched by the profuse presence of your Spirit within me; when my life is guided by my relationship with you, I can't help but express my gratitude by the ways I utilize my resources. May this, then, be a day when I honor you in the variety of ways I give my time, talents, gifts, service, and witness.

Throughout the day, help me be still and know that you are God. And, in the stillness of *this* moment, guide me by your Holy Spirit. Direct me in the path you would have me go so that others might be touched, and healed, and forever transformed because you have used me to your glory.

Loving Lord, help me see the day as a clean slate, a blank canvas that is simply awaiting the Master's touch. I don't know how you're going to do it, but I am so excited by the promise that this ordinary day will be changed into an extraordinary masterpiece because I have chosen to follow you and allow *your* abundance to write upon the hearts of others by employing *my* hands and feet— *my* voice and actions.

Lord, I stand in awe of you and my heart is filled with joy because you have not only called me your child and disciple, but your partner. Where will you send me? What will you create through me? I have no idea what the future holds, but I am *so* very glad that there is certainty that *you* are the One who holds that future—and the One who holds *me* in the palm of your hand!

Thanks be to God! Amen.

Day 16

READ: Exodus 17:1-13

REFLECT:
    With whom are you contending?
    Who is holding your arms up?

RECORD:

_____

_____

_____

_____

_____

_____

_____

_____

_____

_____

_____

_____

_____

_____

_____

PRAY:

Precious Lord, how grateful I am to tiptoe into your presence, knowing that you meet me in this place, just as you continue to meet all who call upon you for protection, deliverance, direction. When I think of the blessings of human deliverance and protection, I am reminded that they come at a price. When our country has been embroiled in war and conflict, brave men and women have continued to put themselves in harm's way for *my* benefit and for the sake of this nation. Thank you for their sacrifice. Thank you for the gift of those who are willing to stand in the gap for others, doing for us what we are unable or unwilling to do for ourselves.

Yet, even as I pray for our veterans, I long for that day when their work is unnecessary; when their sacrifice is no longer required. But until that day, may these and all who serve so faithfully be a reminder that none of us can make it in this world alone. For that reason, you call us to be the body, your body, sharing our unique gifts with one another, and relying on others to walk beside us when we find ourselves in places we don't want to go. For surely life has a way of throwing curve balls at me: illnesses, loss, the betrayal of friends, financial setbacks. And, sometimes it's all I can do just to suit up or show up. That's exactly when you provide those designated hitters—friends and neighbors and *strangers* who raise me up and give me hope. Never let me be too proud to receive those messengers—to rest in their blessing, and to marvel at how you truly work even my weaknesses for good. So, whether I'm in the first or the ninth inning of my life, or anywhere else in between, Lord, continue to move me out of the dugout; empty me out of the bleachers, and use me to radiate your glory.

As Aaron ensured the Israelites' victory by holding up Moses' arms, so may *my* victory today be established in raised hands and a humble heart.

I love you, Lord. Amen.

$$Day\ 17$$

READ: Matthew 8:18-22
Luke 9:18-26

REFLECT:

What do I need to lay down so that I can pick up the cross of Christ?

What have I done, said, or left undone that would indicate that I am unwilling to follow Jesus or that I feel "ashamed" of him?

When have I experienced "paying the price" of being a follower of Jesus? Give thanks for that opportunity and see it as a blessing rather than a slight or condemnation!

RECORD:

PRAY:

Loving Lamb of God, how joyfully I welcome you—lifting my voice in praise and recognizing that you, alone, can save. Joyfully, that is, until I also recognize there is a cost to my decision to follow. For your Word declares that if we are to be first, we must be first in humility, in loving, and in service. If we are to boast, it must be in what you have done—in and through and *for* us. So may your triumphal entry today be into my heart. As I proclaim Hosanna—oh save us—may it be salvation from myself and my selfish ways; from my arrogance and self-centered thoughts; from actions that I use to build myself up while tearing others down, and from my blindness that refuses to see the plight of the lost, the lonely, and the unloved whom I encounter every day. Lord, in your mercy, enter also into the lives of those who are assailed by chronic pain, physical infirmities, dreaded diagnoses. In your will and by your hand, touch, repair and restore—not only physical health, but unfaltering hope; hope that does not disappoint. Rekindle relationships, refresh my soul, and reignite my passion for the possible. Place your hedge of protection around those who keep us safe and by your Spirit guide those who guide this nation.

Recognizing that you call me to yourself, rather than to be enmeshed in the snares of this world, change my perspective on adversity. May I see with *your* eyes this day and rejoice when I have the courage to live as you taught, instead of following after the world. Help me choose the right path in spite of how others might respond. If for this day only, may I recognize the depths of your love for me. And, in that knowledge, may my entire being be filled with rejoicing as I go through my day!

Glory to God! Amen.

Day 18

READ: Matthew 5:1-10

REFLECT:
When do you feel blessed?
How does that line up with Jesus' understanding?

RECORD:

_____

_____

_____

_____

_____

_____

_____

_____

_____

_____

_____

_____

_____

_____

_____

_____

PRAY:

Amazing God, truly, *all* good and perfect gifts come from you. So I pause to thank you—to worship you—to recognize your gift of selfless love by which I have been set free. And, I intentionally stop to give thanks for those who have played an integral part in maintaining the freedom of this nation; for men and women who have loved mercy and country more than the seeming security of hearth and home. Thank you for first responders who bravely face natural and manmade disasters so that others might be safe. This day, comfort those who mourn the loss of those countless heroes who, in offering themselves for the safety and security of others, have gained an eternal home among the faithful cloud of witnesses who stand to cheer us on. For your Word proclaims there *is* no greater love than to lay down one's life so that others might live.

Lord, even as I stop to remember the fallen, I also pray for those who continue to protect and defend at home and abroad. Please fill them with your Spirit and allow your mercy to blot out the horrors of what they must experience and endure. By your Spirit, so permeate every leader—here and abroad that peace would become the new normal and love the guiding principle for *all* peoples. Grant healing to those who live with the ravages of war; comfort to those who mourn the fallen; restoration to relationships stretched to the breaking point, and peace in the midst of our times of transition. Bless those who journey into the next chapter of their lives. And, in all things, O God, cause me to know the incredible way that you continue to provide for me in the mundane and in the magnificent. With that recognition, may I choose to humble myself, forgiving slights, living sacrificially, and loving others in your name.

For it is in that name I pray. Amen.

Day 19

READ: 2 Peter 1:5-11
Galatians 5:19-26

REFLECT:

On what or whom are you waiting today? Is your patience
running thin?

Think about a time when you grew impatient and decided
to act on your own. What happened? Would you change
anything? What lesson might you learn from your
experience?

How is the fruit of patience being lived out in your life?

RECORD:

PRAY:

Timeless Lord, your Word proclaims that a single day is like a thousand years to you and a thousand years like a day. Do you grow tired waiting on us? Waiting for *me* to turn and follow—to trust that *your* timing really is perfect? Did that day on the cross feel like years as you suffered for me, proving your love with nail-scarred hands and a sorrow-filled heart that burst, not from the physical attacks of those who unleashed their anger upon you, but from the deep sorrow of denial; denial from those who proclaimed their love and faithfulness?

When I grow impatient, are you reminded of Judas who simply wanted to speed your triumph along—who so longed for answers and action that he forgot your timing is perfect?

"Wait on the Lord; be strong and take heart, and he *shall* strengthen your heart," the Psalmist implores. So, Lord, I claim those words today. Help me to live moment by moment. Each time I grow impatient, let me be moved to prayer, rather than to panic. Bring to my mind *all* the times you have provided just the right answer at just the right time. As I wait, let me crawl into your lap and feel your gracious, loving arms surround me, assuring me that nothing escapes your notice and that, in the fullness of time, your answers will bring forth more than I could ever imagine. For that's how you love me—gently, perfectly, and with great patience.

So, wait with me, and let me experience you in the waiting. Perhaps, I'll discover that our time together is even better than those things, those answers, those relationships that I've grown impatient waiting on!

Hear my prayer and help me feel your presence as you stay with me in the waiting. Amen.

Day 20

READ: Psalm 30
            Philippians 4:4-7

REFLECT:
> How many ways has God "lifted you up" in the past week?
>   Take time now to list them.
> When has God turned your mourning to dancing?
> How might you rejoice in the Lord this very moment, even as
>   you come to this time of prayer?

RECORD:

PRAY:

Gracious God, Loving Lord, and Sustaining Spirit, it is impossible to contain my joy because of your great love for me. You re-create, cradle, and care for me even in my darkest moments. In times when I'm my most unlovable, you refuse to unleash your anger, choosing instead to call me by name and lead me home. Every moment of every day *you* celebrate *me*! How awesome is your love! How vast your compassion and provision!

So, how could I help but rejoice? How can I see skies of gray when you paint them with your magnificent strokes of grace? How could my cup ever be half empty when you cause it to overflow with beauty for ashes, strength for fear, and joy for mourning? As the day unfolds before me, you unfurl your robe of glory and it fills this place. You roll back the darkness of doubt and despair; you whisper my name and I am filled with your presence! How can such an ordinary person in the midst of such ordinary circumstances be so encompassed by your glorious Light? How can one such as I be so permeated by a ceaseless love that asks nothing in return?

Today, Lover of my soul, let that joy resound in and through my life. May my words be encouraging and edifying; may my eyes recognize those who need a touch of joy; may my feet be swift to convey resources and relief; and may my arms be agents of abundant generosity and gentle grace. Then, even as day fades into night, may this joy and the sure knowledge of your love never fade. Fill me with your Spirit and empty me of my self-centered ways so that rejoicing becomes second nature and jubilation is my only response to life.

Send me out, Lord, and let the Son shine forth from me! Amen.

Day 21

READ: Luke 15:11-31

REFLECT:

Who have I been this week: the wayward child? The unforgiving brother? Or the gracious father?

Today, who do I *choose* to be and how will I live out that choice?

Who has been a father to me? Give thanks to God for that experience…and give thanks to those men in your life who have demonstrated God's forgiveness and extravagant love.

RECORD:

PRAY:

Holy God, on this day I celebrate fathers and I honor *you*. With a grateful heart, I give you thanks and proclaim the truth that, indeed, I have the most perfect parent possible in you, my *Heavenly* Father. For it is you alone who created us in your image and loved us even before we were born. It is *you* who continues to call us your sons and daughters. And, now I begin this day giving thanks that regardless of my *earthly* circumstances, I can be sure that I have been chosen, and loved, and forgiven. So, when, like the prodigal I stray, cause me to hear and heed your call to come home. In those times that I choose to be like the older brother, turning my back on everything I have, complaining about my lack, instead of rejoicing in my abundance, cause me, instead, to have a heart filled with gratitude—a heart that recognizes that richness and rightly attributes all I have to you.

Today, gracious God, I ask a special blessing for earthly fathers. Those who love us beyond measure; those who having no biological children called us their own; for the men who teach us what it means to love and be loved—who make the hard choices so that their children grow in knowledge, wisdom, and in favor with you. For the men—and women—who play *both* parenting roles, for the ones whose work carries them far from home, and for those who are called to protect and defend so that all children might be safe. O God, forgive those fathers who deny or abuse their fatherhood. Call *them* to yourself so that their hearts might be changed and their paths altered, walking, instead by your design and in your will.

As I turn homeward this morning, Lord, may it be a journey grounded in grace through the work of my hands and the gifts from my heart.

This I pray in the name of Jesus, the Christ. Amen.

Day 22

READ: Jeremiah 29:10-14
        Psalm 127:1-2

REFLECT:

    What is holding you captive today?
    How is your self-doubt imprisoning you?
    What does the Lord want to build in you today?
    If you are trapped in thinking about what you "can't do,"
        rather than what *God* can accomplish through you, where
        is your focus?

RECORD:

_____

_____

_____

_____

_____

_____

_____

_____

_____

_____

_____

_____

PRAY:

Lord, I come to this time with you filled with self-doubt; wanting to change so many things about myself; focused on all those abilities and characteristics that *others* display so effortlessly. I long to be so much more than I am—at least, by the world's standards. But here I am, questioning my worth, second-guessing my purpose, wondering where I go from here. Can I really do what others ask of me, or, more importantly, what you ask? You know my struggles; you know the deep, hidden things that have brought me to this place of self-doubt. There are so many reasons not to put myself out there; so many times that my overtures have been rebuffed, my efforts gone unnoticed, my words fallen on deaf ears. What are you teaching me? How do you want me to move beyond my narrow, self-based focus? And, how will you help me do that? Am I the only one who feels so incapable—so defeated? Yet, in my heart I know I am more than a conqueror because you have conquered death and darkness.

Truly, I don't have a clue how you're going to use me. But I'm asking you to help me have the courage to trust that you will. By your Spirit, direct my eyes heavenward, move my heart homeward, still me, and return me to your Word. You *do* know the plans you have for me! You created and formed me by your perfect design and you want to use me just as I am—for those purposes for which I was created! Transform my self-doubt through confidence in the truth that I am *your* child, and as a child of God, I *can* do all things through Christ, who will continue to strengthen me. If only for today, I choose to walk in that reality. I choose to gather my self-assurance from you, knowing that you are building in me the image of Christ.

Holy Daddy, I give thanks that the family resemblance can be found in *me* more and more every day!! Amen.

Day 23

READ: Psalm 100
　　　2 Corinthians 4:7-15

REFLECT:

For what do you give thanks to God today?

Being a sheep also means that we have a shepherd. In what ways do you need to be led, fed, and protected today? Give thanks that the Good Shepherd will do it for you!

How are you feeling "hard pressed, perplexed, or struck down"? How is God's grace in these temporary circumstances enabling thanksgiving to abound in you?

RECORD:

PRAY:

Gracious God, you journey with us. When we ascend to the heights of celebration or go to the place of deepest despair, you walk with us. Even when we travel to every place in between, by your Word, you promise never to leave or forsake us. Thank you that in those times when we choose the wide path, the lure of what will soon fade, the search for fool's gold, by your Spirit you gently woo us back, providing a way of escape and pointing to the narrow road that leads to a life that is abundant.

So, I ask you to lead me a little farther today, Lord. I ask that you would move me to the place of gratitude and thanksgiving. I pray that you would cause me to see the abundance, rather than any perceived lack, already filling my life. And, in those times when I am hard pressed, perplexed or struck down, let it be for *your* sake. Let it be because I have stood firm for you, rejoicing in my salvation and boasting in you instead of what I think *I've* done on my own. When I can find no reason to give thanks, bring to my mind the promised victory over this life as I am caught up with you in glory.

Until that time, my Traveling Companion, let praise and thanksgiving always be the first response on my lips. Let my heart be filled with gratitude and my eyes alight with the joy that comes only from you. In *all* things I *will* rejoice because I know that it is your will for me and I am certain that even my most sacrificial days lived for you pale in comparison to the selfless way you have loved and provided for me.

Today, I will celebrate! Today, I will give thanks with my whole being! Today, my gratitude for your grace will overshadow *any* grief! Today, be glorified in my praise. Amen.

Day 24

READ: Psalm 38:13-22
Romans 5:1-5
I Corinthians 13:1-7

REFLECT:

What have you refused to hear or speak? Who do you feel is
your adversary this day?

In the past, how has God rushed to come to your rescue? Are
there foes or circumstances from which you need to be
rescued now?

What is "difficulty" producing in you today? Despair or
hope—depression or joy?

When has hope in Christ led you to higher ground? When
has your hope not been a disappointment? How might you
apply that hope to your current circumstances?

RECORD:

_____

_____

_____

_____

_____

_____

_____

_____

PRAY:

Lord, be not far from me today because it seems you are the only friend I have. I have been maligned, mocked, and misunderstood. My best intentions have been misconstrued and my cries of protest are met with scorn. Hopeless and helpless, I have been reduced to silence, stillness, and solitude.

But that's when you make your presence known to me, Lord, for when I finally take the time to be silent, your still, small voice speaks volumes. When I plummet to the depths, you pick me up—raise me up in the hope of your Word. And in my isolation, I find I'm not really alone at all. In the highest highs and the lowest lows, you are there. In seclusion and in the midst of the multitudes, you are there. Thank you; thank you for loving me enough to be my constant companion. Thank you for the lesson of Romans 8 that we *can* hope for what we don't see as we wait for it with perseverance. And in that hope, I can be assured that you will work even this time—even this circumstance together for good because I love you and I *know* I am called according to *your* purpose. *Your* hope will not disappoint and *your* love will never fail!

So, as I wait, let it be with a heart filled with love, and in the certainty that love hopes and endures *all* things. Remind me that any slight, conflict, or betrayal I might experience is diminished when placed alongside the injustices and indignities you endured. Help me recall that you are no stranger to what I'm going through.

Taking you at your word, I *will* choose hope today; for my hope is built in you, my Savior and my Lord. Through the power of Jesus' name I pray. Amen.

Day 25

READ: Ezekiel 36:22-28
  Romans 6:1-6
  Colossians 3:8-11

REFLECT:

God promises the Israelites a new heart. How has *your* heart been renewed lately?

How has God's Spirit caused you to walk in newness of life? What might you do today to celebrate what God has done for you?

How has God made you new? Are there still things that need to be shed?

In what ways are you looking more like Christ?

RECORD:

PRAY:

Ever-Creating, Ever-Renewing Lord, as new life bursts forth all around me, so you come and create in me something new, good, and revitalized. You take the barrenness of my stone-cold heart and transform it into fertile ground where your Word is deeply planted. And from that place, fresh understandings spring forth. You remove the lethargy of days and the fatigue of nights, and renew my focus so that *my* desires begin to align with *your* will. You coax forth the fruit of your Spirit in my life as I throw off the mantle of wintry desolation and take up the easy cloak of compliance with what you have in store for me.

It's *good* to be alive! So good to be your child and to bask in the warmth of your Son! You have restored my soul and sealed me from harm's way; you have kept your promises, provided for me *everything* I needed, and held back those things that would only cause me harm or grief. It's only now, in the light of this new day, that I recognize such faithfulness; only now in the birth of this new season that my vision has cleared enough to see the vastness of your mercy and your love.

Surely, you make all things new! Truly, you are recreating *me*— moment by moment—in your image. What a blessing and what a beautiful picture of your kingdom to come. May the lessons of this season not be forgotten, and my blossoming passion for the possible not fade away. As a child eagerly reaches for her father when learning to walk, so I reach for the safety of your tender hand, knowing that you will keep me from falling. For I need you, Lord, as I step into this day with all of its possibilities.

Keep me laughing; keep me loving; keep me moving in your direction—with joy in my heart and a spring in my step! Amen.

Day 26

READ: Psalm 42:1-11
　　　Luke 24:13-35

REFLECT:

When have you found your "soul downcast"? With what
　　disappointment or disillusion have you been dealing?
How does the Psalmist deal with his despair? How might you?
Why were the two on the road to Emmaus disappointed?
　　What changed their perspective? How was Jesus made
　　known to them? How did they respond?
How has Jesus been made known to you? How might you
　　respond in that knowledge?

RECORD:

_____

_____

_____

_____

_____

_____

_____

_____

_____

_____

PRAY:

Lord, your Word tells me that you know everything. You know where I am—physically and spiritually. You see when I come out, and when I go in. You know when I rage against you and when I am simply too weary to be angry with anyone or anything. And, that's where I find myself today. Simply weary, worn out, worried out, and wondering what's coming next. Why, Lord? Why can I feel so right with the world one moment and the next instant be assailed by despair? Why do past memories keep me imprisoned and hold such power over me? Why do I find myself on this emotional roller coaster with no end to the ride in sight? And, what was it in this latest event that has taken me back so many years? What has taken hold of me and transported me back to a time when I was powerless, having no idea of the strength available to me through you? Even now, I feel like those two on the road who walked with the sight of the world—so despondent and so filled with the belief that their hopes and dreams had been dashed by a cross-shaped enemy.

Yet, even then you were there—just as you are here now. So, open my eyes as you opened theirs. Remind me of the treasure found in your holy Word: that you watch over me, keep me from all harm, preserve my soul, and guard my going out and coming in, today and always! Like those first disciples, may I find joy in your provision and strength in your salvation. In that truth, disappointment *can* be overcome with delight, and despondency eradicated with dancing. In *you* I find reasons for rejoicing and the power to overcome the past!

So bring on the day because I know that you have begun a good work in me. I believe you will continue refining me through this and all circumstances until the day of your return. Bring it on, Lord! Amen.

Day 27

READ: Jeremiah 9:23-24
        Acts 7:32-33
        I Thessalonians 5:12-24

REFLECT:

What have you found yourself boasting about apart from God?
How might the God of peace bring peace into your midst today?
Who are you being called to comfort? Who needs your prayers?

RECORD:

PRAY:

Gracious God, as I meet you here today, I recognize that I am standing upon Holy Ground, standing upon the Rock, Christ Jesus. I am certain that I *can* stand only because you have called me to be your child—not bragging about what I have or who I am, but boasting about *your* unfathomable ability to take common, ordinary lives and transform them into extraordinary ministry. Here I stand in conjunction with all those called to be your church—set apart, not for arrogance, but for an air of humility, knowing that I have been blessed to be a blessing to everyone I encounter. And here I stand, so grateful to you, for calling and equipping me. By your hand, you have led me that I might lead others. By your Spirit, you filled me with wisdom and compassion, causing me to love in your name even those that the world deems unlovable. For that's what it means to be a part of your faithful Body, as I live out your command to love you and to love others.

Lord, I also stand on your invitation to prayer. In these uncertain and ever-changing times, help me draw strength from the One who is the same yesterday, today, and tomorrow, for I know, O God, that in order to be able to stand at all, I must first fall—fall on my knees and seek your face.

With those first disciples, may I see you clearly as the Christ— Son of the Living God, and by faith may I move beyond a reliance on staid and stale religion into a revelation that reflects the wideness of your mercy. Fill this place with your Spirit; fill *me* with your Spirit that I might be compelled to go and fill this world with your unconditional love. Fill this day with opportunities to live for you as I pray this, and all things, in Jesus' name. Amen.

Day 28

READ: Isaiah 6:1-8
John 19:1-3
Revelation 7:9-17 and 22:20

REFLECT:

When was the last time you were willing to say, "Here I am, send me!"? Did God take you seriously? Into what adventure did God lead you? When was the last time you chose not to answer God's call, "Whom shall I send?"

How did Jesus' enemies mock him? What is the irony in the title they gave him? What is the difference between the way the Good Shepherd was "honored" on earth and in heaven? What does God promise to do with our tears?

RECORD:

PRAY:

Holy, holy, holy Lord, God of power and might, heaven and earth are filled with your glory. Hosanna in the highest. Blessed is He who comes in the name of the Lord. Hosanna in the highest.[2]

Hosanna, oh save us, Lord, for we truly are a people of unclean lips in a land of unclean thoughts and deeds. Save *me*, for too often I'm like those who mocked the One who only sought to serve and to save those of us who are held captive by our own thoughts and the direction of this crass and uncaring world. Like a stupid sheep, I wander away, fooled by what seems to be greener meadows. And, like a loving Shepherd, you search until you find me; call until I respond; and lovingly lead me to lush pastures where my soul is restored through your gift of reconciliation. How blessed I am, and how ungrateful I can be!

Yet, you promise victory, and as I lift my eyes to gaze into the purity of yours, I am assured that you will never let me go. So with the cloud of faithful witnesses and all the multitude of heaven, I choose to proclaim, "We give you thanks, Lord God Almighty. Blessing and honor and glory and power be to him who sits on the throne, and to the Lamb, forever and ever!"

The Spirit and the bride say, "Come!" And you invite all who thirst to come and to freely partake of the Water of Life. So, parched, I turn homeward as I cry out to you this day, "Even so, come, Lord Jesus—come quickly!" Amen.

---

2 From the communion liturgy published in *The United Methodist Hymnal*, Abingdon Press, 2001.

Day 29

READ: John 8:31-36
Galatians 4:31-5:1

REFLECT:

From what has Christ released you?

What are you doing to set others free from the bonds of guilt, despair, hopelessness, financial entrapment?

What is God *calling* you to do?

RECORD:

PRAY:

Loving Lord, thank you for your living Word. Thank you for the promise that "whom the Son has set free, is free indeed." That, like the Israelites, you have led our ancestors to a place of religious freedom, given strength to those colonists who sought to maintain their place in this land, provided healing for this fractured nation when brother fought against brother, and kept us strong even when the tyranny of other nations determined to dehumanize and devour all means of freedom. But, God, I know that it is *for* freedom that you set me free: freedom *from* fear and freedom *to* access your throne of grace, so that I might be in relationship with you; to *live* as one who is free in Christ, not using my freedom as a cover-up for evil, but for serving others in your name. So hold back my foolishness when I try to be free from you, and stay my steps when I try to escape from your will and from your ways. Remind me and remind this nation, as often as necessary, that *might* does not serve to make us *right*, and that we will never be truly free until all people are released from their bonds of unbelief, poverty, persecution, subservience, and ignorance.

Bless those who labor in your name to set the captive free. Surround with your hedge of protection those who continue to protect and defend us. Have mercy on those who would enslave others, and change their hearts so that *they* may be set free from what ensnares them. Gracious God, forgive me when my focus is on myself, rather than you and when I squander the profuse blessings you shower upon me. Hear my cries and come, Lord. Come and heal my foolish heart. Come, Lord, and heal our land!!

This I pray in agreement with your Spirit and your Word. Amen.

Day 30

READ: Luke 9:23-26
Luke 14:25-35
Acts 2:41-47

REFLECT:

What does a modern day disciple look like?

What are some ways you demonstrate that you are a follower
of Jesus Christ? In what ways do you fellowship with
other Christians? Are you always in "one accord"? How is
fellowship restored once it is broken?

Are you a "pot stirrer" or a "peace maker"? How do you
increase your knowledge of God?

RECORD:

_____

_____

_____

_____

_____

_____

_____

_____

_____

_____

PRAY:

Loving Lord, I'm reminded that I'm simply a clay vessel—imperfect and sometimes a bit cracked! But you fill your vessels with the Word who became flesh. In that Word, I've discovered that you not only came to live among us generations ago, but in this present age you also have given me sight to recognize you and a heart to receive you. Yet, my journey is far from over, for you promise that your Word will not return empty and that through *me* it must go forth. By your Holy Spirit, then, use me—my faithfulness, my wisdom, my God-given gifts—to accomplish your purposes. For it is your good pleasure that none should perish, but that all should have eternal life. As I forgive, serve, extend hospitality, become a good steward, the entire world has an opportunity to see what it *really* means to live abundantly. So, today may my light shine before others in such a way that it's obvious that any of my good thoughts or words or deeds hasn't been completed under my own power, but through the power of the risen Christ. Give me words to explain the reason for my hope, and move me to excitement in sharing the great Good News of your endless love—for that is what true discipleship means.

Keep me mindful of those you place before me today and remind me that my weakness is perfected in your strength. Should I forget *whose* I am, cause me to know that I am *your* royal priesthood, *your* workmanship created to do good works which are initiated and completed in love. Today, I choose *you* as my model and my guide because today and every day, you have chosen *me* to be the one who will carry your light into this dark and dying world.

Today, I am willing and I am yours! This is my prayer for my blessed Savior's sake. Amen.

Day 31

READ: John 3:1-20
James: 1:16-18
1 Peter 1:3-9
John 1:1-5

REFLECT:

What led Nicodemus to believe Jesus came from God? Was Nicodemus being led by sight or by faith?

What was God's purpose for sending Jesus into our world? What is the condemnation of the world?

How has the Light illumined *your* world? How might you let that Light shine through you today?

RECORD:

_____

_____

_____

_____

_____

_____

_____

_____

_____

_____

PRAY:

O holy God, in every season, may we remember that night long ago—one in which there was no room. Yet, into circumstances such as ours, to people such as us, the Christ child was born. Giving up your heavenly home, you came to live among us so that we might know what it is to *truly* live. You came as a helpless baby, that we might know help is simply a prayer away. You came as a meek child, that we might discover the power of humility. You came in the darkness of night that we might know the glory of your Light—a light that banishes the darkness and breaks the bonds of all that would seek to ensnare us. Today, may I be bathed in that Light as I look to the day of rejoicing in your return. Today be born again in me—that I might face such a world as this with hope, joy, and peace as increasingly I become an instrument of your love.

As you gave to us your most precious gift of Jesus Christ, so today may I return to you that which I hold most dear: my time, my talents, and resources—my very life so that this greatest story ever told becomes *my* story, one that is shared in this community and beyond.

Today, dear Lord, may all that I think, do, and say be tangible and obvious signs that there *is* room within my heart, and that you have, indeed, been born in me!

This is my prayer through Christ Jesus, my Lord. Amen.